Championing Humanity: Dorothea Dix's Trailblazing Impact

MARKO D

Copyright © 2023 Marko D

All rights reserved.

ISBN:9798861234108

Table of Contents

Acknowledgments... 4

Introduction:
The Silent Crusader - Understanding Dorothea Dix........................... 6

Chapter 1:
Early Life - The Crucible Of Character... 9
    Birth and Family Background... 9
    Childhood Struggles and Formative Influences............................ 11
    The role of her grandmother, Dorothea Lynde............................ 14

Chapter 2:
A Mind Of Her Own - The Educational Years................................... 17
    Early Schooling and Self-Education... 17
    Her stint as a teacher and school founder............................... 20

Chapter 3:
The Turning Point - A Visit to the Asylum...................................... 23
    The Fateful Visit to the Massachusetts Prison........................... 23
    First-Hand Accounts of Appalling Conditions............................. 27

Chapter 4:
The Awakening - Dix's Moral Imperative....................................... 30
    The realization of her mission... 30
    Initial Attempts at Advocacy... 32

Chapter 5:
The Battlefront - Lobbying the Legislatures................................... 36
    Her Memorial to the Massachusetts Legislature......................... 36
    The Persuasive Power of Her Reports..................................... 39

Table of Contents

Chapter 6:
Victory & Vexation - Policy Triumphs And Obstacles 42
    Successes in Law Reform 42
    The Final Act: Life After Advocacy 50

Chapter 7:
Expanding Horizons - Beyond America's Borders 52
    Her impact on European mental health care reform 53
    Policy Shifts: The American Domino Effect vs. The European Tapestry 56

Chapter 8:
The Collaborators - Friends And Foes 58
    The Harmony of Dix and Samuel Gridley Howe 58
    Conflicts and alliances 67

Chapter 9:
The Civil War Years - Dix As Superintendent Of Army Nurses 68
    Her role in the Union Army 68
    Challenges and controversies 74

Chapter 10:
The Final Mile - Dix's Later Years 77
    Retrospective of Her Impact 78
    Her legacy in the modern era 82
    People and circumstances that contributed to her journey 86

Notes and References
Where The Story Meets The Street 90

Acknowledgments

Where do you even begin with acknowledgements, right? Well, Dorothea Dix couldn't have been the icon she was without a supporting cast. Hats off to her era, the 1800s, a time buzzing with reformist energy. Could she have become who she was without those societal winds? Doubtful.

Family matters, too. Her parents may not have been ideal, but they lit the initial spark. Would her push for reform be as passionate without her strict upbringing? It's the age-old question of nature versus nurture.

How can we not mention the role models and mentors like her grandmother, Dorothea Lynde, who gave her stability and education? These early influences set the stage for the change-maker she'd become. And let's not overlook the disadvantaged folks she met along the way, the forgotten people who nudged her into advocacy. A single visit to a Massachusetts prison sparked it all. Makes you ponder, what game-changing moments are we missing in our own lives?

Kudos to her contemporaries, Samuel Gridley Howe, Horace Mann, and others. They were more than friends; they were collaborators in a shared mission. And a nod to the lawmakers who heeded her calls. They turned her appeals into real, tangible change.

So, who deserves the credit for Dorothea Dix's legacy? It's not just her; it's a chorus of voices and influences. It's proof that the story of one person's impact is rarely a solo act. A lesson for us all.

Introduction

The Silent Crusader - Understanding Dorothea Dix

Have you ever stopped to consider the world of the 1800s? It was an era of paradoxes, a mixture of enlightenment and ignorance. Within this world walked Dorothea Lynde Dix, a woman not born of privilege or incredible power but of an ordinary life that she turned into an extraordinary mission. Why should you care about her? If you've ever considered the importance of mental health or the dignity of human life, you've stepped into her influence.

We often celebrate the movers and shakers standing on podiums, leading armies, or inventing gadgets that change our lives overnight. But what about those who move in the quiet? Dorothea Dix was one of those silent crusaders. No, she didn't invent a machine or write a constitution. What she did was far more challenging: she changed minds. Not accessible minds but those set in the unyielding stone of 19th-century societal norms.

Dorothea's story doesn't begin with grandeur or end with extraordinary recognition. It's not a story sprinkled with glitz or glamour. Instead, her story is one of grit, determination, and a relentless fight for the voiceless — particularly for the mentally ill who were cast aside by society. If you think about it, she was a century ahead. At a time when society dismissed mental illness as a moral failing or a hopeless condition, Dix was a torchbearer for change. Can you imagine stepping into filthy, neglected institutions and telling people there's a better way? It's akin to stepping into a dark cave and announcing the discovery of fire.

So, who was this woman who wandered into asylums and spoke with presidents and popes? Was she just a reformer, or can we even dare to say, a prophet of social justice? This isn't just a biography; it's a deep dive into the life of a woman who looked at the neglected corners of society and saw not just despair but possibility. Let's embark on this together if you're up for a journey.

We'll wander through corridors of dimly lit asylums where Dix found her calling. We'll sit in legislative chambers where her voice, though soft, resonated like a bell of change. We'll examine what she did and why she did it. To understand Dorothea is to understand a piece of ourselves — the part that yearns for a better world that sees not problems but solutions in waiting.

She might not have seen the whole fruit of her labour. True, she didn't live in a world of hashtags or viral news that could amplify her message within seconds. But she laid the foundations upon which others would build.

Just like a single stone in an archway isn't the entire structure; without it, the whole thing could collapse. That's Dorothea Dix for you — indispensable yet humble, enduring yet ever so human.

In the following chapters, you'll get to know Dorothea Dix not as a historical footnote but as humanity's living, breathing crusader. You'll see the challenges she faced, the adversaries she subdued, and the lives she touched. And you'll find some of her resilience and vision inside yourself. After all, don't we all have a silent crusade within us waiting to be discovered?

So, are you ready to turn the page and step back into another era? Because as much as this is a story about the past, it's also very much about the present — and the future. Let's get started.

Chapter 1

Early Life - The Crucible Of Character

Let's start from the very beginning, shall we? Because in stories like Dorothea Dix's, origins aren't just footnotes — they're the root system of a towering redwood, feeding every branch, every leaf, every piece of bark that you can see above ground. How does someone go from obscurity to changing the course of American mental health? Let's dig in.

Birth and Family Background

Picture it: Hampden, Maine, in the year 1802. It's not exactly a bustling metropolis, but it's the backdrop for the birth of Dorothea Lynde Dix. Born to Joseph and Mary Dix, you'd think she'd have your average, run-of-the-mill upbringing. But let me tell you, "average" is a term that simply wouldn't stick to her — not now, not ever.

Her father, Joseph, was a Methodist preacher. Sounds respectable enough, right? But hold your horses; the man had his vices. His interest in spirituality was counterbalanced by an affinity for drink and a penchant for the erratic. Her mother, Mary, was plagued by debilitating mental health issues. So, who does the caregiving in a home where the caregivers are, to put it kindly, occupied?

Dorothea. At the tender age of 12, she moved out and lived with her grandmother in Boston. Just let that sink in for a moment. A 12-year-old chose to carve her path because the one laid before her was strewn with obstacles. She didn't know it then, but this early hardship, this pre-teen crucible, forged a character that would make her a powerhouse advocate.

Ever wonder how these early years shaped her? Well, think about it. If you grow up in a house where mental illness and instability are the only constant, two things could happen: you become a statistic or a change agent. Dorothea chose the latter. But how does a young woman, hardly a blip on society's radar, move from the periphery to the epicentre? You could call it fate or divine design; I call it grit wrapped in a cloak of necessity.

The family backdrop is crucial here. It's like soil to a plant. Too alkaline or too acidic, and the plant won't thrive. But some plants adapt; they defy the odds. That's Dorothea. Born in an environment that could easily stunt her growth, she adapted and used those conditions to fuel her lifelong mission.

So why does her early life matter? Because the roots inform the branches. Dorothea's tumultuous upbringing wasn't a side note; it was the prologue, the early shaping of a woman who would stare down senators and challenge societal norms. Her early life challenges didn't define her, but they did fuel her. They were the anvil on which her character was forged, and boy, she turned out to be a formidable character.

Let me ask: Can you think of a single influential figure who hasn't been through the wringer in one way or another? Hardship has a funny way of sanding down our rough edges, revealing the core of who we are. For Dorothea, that core was made of iron will, and a heart big enough to encompass those society had cast aside.

We're just getting started, my friends. Dorothea Dix's early life was a mere prelude to a symphony — a complex, challenging, uplifting composition. Interested in the next movement? Stick around; you won't be disappointed.

Childhood Struggles and Formative Influences

So, we've dipped our toes into the ocean of Dorothea Dix's life, but how about we wade in a bit deeper? Ever think about what shapes a hero? Sure, Superman had Krypton and, well, superpowers. But Dorothea? She had a different fuel, not from distant galaxies but from her early life's inner struggles and external adversities. Let's dissect those, shall we?

By the time she was 12, Dorothea had already moved out of her home—a home that felt like anything but. Why? We've got a father engrossed in a cocktail of theology and inebriation and a mother ensnared by her mind's dark shadows. Imagine growing up like that. Dorothea was dealt a hand that many would fold on if life were a game of poker. But she played her cards, and let's just say she played them well.

In her household, the role of parent and child were reversed. She became a maternal figure for her younger siblings. Can you grasp the gravity of a child being burdened with responsibilities that would crush most adults? Yet, these early scars weren't her downfall; they were the kiln in which her resolve was fired.

When Dorothea moves to Boston to live with her wealthy grandmother, she doesn't just switch physical locations; she steps into a new realm of possibilities. The lady couldn't squander chances; she seized them with both hands. Living in Boston gave her something she never had — a stable home. But it also handed her a quiver full of arrows called "education," "social standing," and "connections." Make no mistake, though; she didn't just use these arrows to shoot for the moon. She aimed right at the societal issues she had lived through.

In Boston, she's introduced to the world of formal education, which for her wasn't just a chalkboard and dusty textbooks. It was her platform, her stage. She began teaching at 14 — yes, you read that right, 14! — and came under the influence of some remarkable mentors. Let's throw some names around, shall we? William Ellery Channing was a unitarian minister who was a prominent advocate for social reform. Sound like someone else we know?

These mentors were like the conductors in the orchestra of her life. They didn't play the instruments but guided her to make music from her skills and unyielding passion. Who would Dorothea be without them? A ship in the harbour is safe, but that's not what ships — or Dorothea Dix — were built for. Her mentors helped her hoist the sails.

Religion and Morality: The Compass Points North

We can only talk about Dix if we talk about her spiritual underpinnings. For her, religion wasn't about Sunday sermons; it was her moral compass. Inspired by the Unitarian values of human dignity and social justice, she laid down the tracks her life-train would run on.

Okay, pause. Why bother with these early struggles and influences? Because they're the recipe for the dynamo that Dorothea became. It's like asking why the foundation of a skyscraper matters. You can't reach for the skies without something solid under your feet, right?

Her childhood struggles didn't just shape her; they propelled her. They were the grindstone against which she sharpened herself. Each struggle carved out a facet of the gem she became, and each influence added lustre to her brilliance.

So what's next? How does a scarred but unbroken young girl, armed with a quiver of newly acquired skills, march into a world desperately needing change? Well, my friend, you'll have to keep reading to find out, but I promise you—it's a tale worth its weight in both tears and triumphs.

The role of her grandmother, Dorothea Lynde

Alright, folks, grab your metaphorical popcorn. We're delving into the role of one particularly extraordinary woman — Dorothea's grandmother, Dorothea Lynde. This lady deserves more than a passing mention, trust me.

Stepping Into The Breach: When Grandma Becomes a Lifeline

Remember that tumultuous household Dix grew up in? Her grandma Dorothea Lynde saw the writing on the wall and said, "Enough is enough!" She swooped in and did what grandmas do best—provided a safety net. The move to Boston wasn't just a change in ZIP code. It was a lifeline thrown to a drowning girl. It was Grandma Lynde who orchestrated this life-changing shift. Why does this matter? Because if life is a maze, then Dix's grandmother gave her a compass and a flashlight.

When Dorothea Dix moved in with her grandma, the young girl found something she'd never had — a natural home. Think about that. The word 'home' might ring simple, but it's a complex cocktail of feelings, isn't it? Safety, warmth, love — all mixed together. And let's not forget education and opportunity, two things Grandma Lynde ensured her granddaughter got a taste of. Her home in Boston wasn't just four walls; it was a launchpad.

Wealth Beyond Riches: Teaching the Value of Social Capital

Now, Grandma Lynde wasn't just wealthy; she was connected. She was what we'd call "old money" today, deeply ingrained in Boston's social and intellectual circles. And guess who got invited to the soirees, the gatherings where big ideas were tossed around like salads at a summer BBQ? That's right, young Dorothea. It's one thing to have money, but to have social currency, ah, that's the secret sauce. Grandma Lynde instilled the unspoken rules of society. She taught her how to network long before LinkedIn made it a buzzword.

What's Good for the Goose: Transferring Values and Traditions

You might be wondering—did these two Dorotheas, separated by a generation, share more than just a name? Oh, you bet. Grandma Lynde was deeply religious, a woman of sturdy moral fibre. Sound familiar? Of course, it does. The elder Dorothea didn't just offer her granddaughter a place to sleep; she passed down a legacy, a framework of values that would guide young Dix for years. We're talking about Unitarian values of social justice, of caring for those less fortunate. This stuff didn't just make Dix the woman she was; it made her the revolutionary she became.

So, What's the Verdict?

Can we say that Dorothea Dix would have been "just another person" without her grandmother? It's a dicey question, isn't it? There's an old saying, "It takes a village to raise a child." Well, sometimes it just takes one person, one solid, unyielding cornerstone, to change the course of a river. In Dix's life, that cornerstone was her grandmother.

The moral compass, social connections, and opportunity for education weren't just stepping stones but building blocks. And they came from Grandma Lynde. She was the sculptor, chiselling away at a block of marble, helping reveal the masterpiece within.

If you ever wonder how a shy, fragile young girl could become a juggernaut of social change, look no further than the influence of a grandmother who wasn't just a namesake but a North Star. It goes to show, doesn't it? Sometimes heroes are made, not just born, and sometimes the making starts with someone who knows just what you're capable of — even when you don't see it yourself.

In the grand scheme of things, Dorothea Lynde — the grandma — was the unsung hero in the epic tale of Dorothea Dix. And like any great hero, her influence and lessons lived on long after her role in the story seemed to end. That's the power of legacy for you, a fire that keeps burning, lighting the way for generations to come. Isn't it something?

Chapter 2

A Mind Of Her Own - The Educational Years

Oh, friends, buckle up! We're diving into the fascinating, maybe even paradoxical, educational journey of Dorothea Lynde Dix. A woman of her time? Hardly. She was aeons ahead, and her education — or sometimes the lack thereof — played a colossal role.

Early Schooling and Self-Education

First, how does a girl in early 19th-century America even get an education? Well, it wasn't a cakewalk, let me tell you. Remember, this era was when women attending college was rarer than a solar eclipse. Dix's family wasn't exactly rolling in money, but they weren't destitute either. What they lacked in financial stability, they made up for in colourful personalities that made every day an adventure.

Dix went to what you'd call a "common school" for her earliest education. Picture this: a one-room schoolhouse filled with kids of different ages and one overworked teacher trying to keep the peace. Sounds like a circus, doesn't it? For many women of her time, a couple of years in such a setting would be the alpha and omega of their educational journey. But we're talking about Dorothea Dix, a woman who seemed to have a lifelong subscription to "I'll do it my way" magazine.

She wasn't exactly thrilled with the primary curriculum and the uninspiring environment. Can you blame her? After all, how many times can you recite the alphabet before wanting to learn, you know, actual stuff?

The Grandma Effect and Self-Education

Grandma Lynde, remember her? She comes back into the picture here. When Dix moved in with her grandma in Boston, she had access to something more enriching than a classroom — a library. And what a game-changer that was. Who needs a school when you've got the wisdom of ages sitting on shelves? Dix took to books like a bee to honey. There's a kind of magic in teaching yourself, isn't there? It's like cooking without a recipe. Sometimes you mess up, but oh, the dishes you can create when you get it right!

Self-education is like sculpting yourself from a block of marble, and boy, did Dix create a masterpiece. Her grandma's library gave her the tools — books on history, philosophy, science — and Dix did the chiselling. We're talking about a woman who would eventually hobnob with legislators, so you better believe she wouldn't settle for being 'just another woman' of her time.

School's Out, Life's In The Real World Becomes a Classroom

At a ridiculously young age — 14, Dix started teaching. You heard that right. Fourteen. Imagine being a teenager and running your own school. It's like playing a video game in expert mode from the get-go! Yet, she was teaching other kids, sharing bookish knowledge, life skills, values, and stuff you don't find in textbooks.

Life was her classroom in this phase, and her challenges were pop quizzes. How do you manage a classroom? How do you get people to take you seriously when you're not old enough to vote? She learned folks. She learned through trial and fire, through errors and triumphs. Isn't that the best way to learn, though? There are no cushioned classrooms, no safety nets, just life in all its messy glory.

A Self-Made Scholar

So, what's the takeaway here? Did Dix miss out by not going to a prestigious university? I dare say no. She was her own university. She took her formal education fragments and built upon them like a maestro. Sometimes, the most excellent teachers are the students who teach themselves.

Ever heard of the phrase, "When life gives you lemons, make lemonade"? Dorothea Dix didn't just make lemonade; she set up a whole empire, intellectually speaking. She might not have been a college graduate, but she was a graduate of the School of Hard Knocks, and she graduated summa cum laude. Now, if that's not education, what is?

Dix didn't just break the mould; she smashed it to smithereens. Her self-education allowed her to converse with intellectuals, write persuasively, and argue coherently. How many of us can say we're self-taught and then go on to influence national policy? Only a few, but Dix did. So, next time you think about education, remember Dorothea

Dix—sometimes the best schools have no walls, and the best teachers have no degrees. Notable, isn't it?

Her stint as a teacher and school founder

So, you remember that Dix was just 14 when she started teaching? Let's unpack that, shall we? How does a teenager, barely out of childhood herself, take on the Herculean task of moulding young minds? Imagine being thrown into the deep end of a pool, but it's filled with rambunctious kids instead of water. Sounds overwhelming. But remember, we're talking about Dorothea Lynde Dix here — a woman who never met a challenge she didn't like.

Opening Her Own School: Crazy or Genius?

Now, if you thought her becoming a teacher was jaw-dropping, wait till you hear this: she opened her own school at 19! You know that saying about how entrepreneurs are the rock stars of the business world? Well, Dix was like the Mick Jagger of 19th-century educators.

Why did she decide to open a school? Could the formal structures be too constricting for her expansive mind? Or maybe she wanted to set the tone of education that she felt was missing in her life. You see, Dix was never one to settle for "good enough." For her, it was go big or go home.

Her school was unique in so many ways. Let's start with the fact that she took in both rich and poor students, charging fees from those who could afford it and teaching the underprivileged for free. Have you ever been to a concert where they have both VIP and general sections, but the atmosphere makes everyone feel like a rock star? That's what Dix's school was like — where social divides crumbled.

The Curriculum: A Reflection of Dix's Own Learning

Have you ever met someone so magnetic that you wonder if they have a gravity field? Dix was that person. The subjects taught in her school were a potpourri of traditional and revolutionary. Basic subjects like reading and writing? Sure. But she also included moral and ethical lessons, shaped perhaps by the disarray she had experienced in her family life. Remember, Dix was largely self-taught, and the knowledge she had gained from her reading adventures spilt over into her teaching. She wasn't just filling young heads with facts but shaping character. How's that for educational reform?

Struggles and Triumphs: The Roller Coaster Ride

The journey wasn't without its bumps. Money was tight. A school is not just about students and teachers; it's about managing a space, securing resources, dealing with parents — you get the drill. Dix was the captain of this ship, and sometimes the seas were rough. But did she abandon the ship? Never.

Think of it like hiking up a steep mountain; you're going to trip, maybe even sprain an ankle. But the view from the top? Absolutely worth it. And let's not forget the rich life experiences she was gathering; they became the gold mine for her later activism.

How Teaching Shaped the Activist in Dix

While Dix's journey as a teacher and school founder was monumental in its own right, it was also a preamble to her later work. If we consider her life like a well-written novel, then her educational stint was the chapter that set the stage for the climax — her sweeping crusade for mental health reform.

She developed essential skills like public speaking, effective communication, and the art of persuasion — all of which would later serve her well in the corridors of power. Imagine learning to play guitar for fun and later discovering that you're a natural at it. Dix's educational endeavours had prepared her for a much larger stage, and what a performance it would be!

Through the challenges and triumphs, Dix continued to be a student herself. She was like an artist who's always satisfied with their masterpiece, constantly revising, adding a stroke here, erasing a line there. Every interaction, every struggle, and every success was another brushstroke on the canvas of her life. Ever wonder why some people never seem to age mentally? It's because they never stop learning.

So, was Dorothea Lynde Dix a successful teacher and school founder? Absolutely. But more than that, she was a lifelong learner. And isn't that the best kind of teacher? The one who acknowledges that the learning process never ends, not for the student and the master.

Chapter 3

The Turning Point - A Visit to the Asylum

Isn't life full of moments that change everything? You know, those seemingly ordinary days that, upon a single twist, can set us on a path we never envisioned. Dorothea Dix had one such moment. A visit that forever changed her life and, indeed, the lives of countless others. Let's delve into that chapter, shall we?

The Fateful Visit to the Massachusetts Prison

Picture this: You walk into a room thinking you're about to conduct a simple Sunday school class and walk out with a life mission that would make even superheroes blink. Sounds like something out of a novel. But for Dorothea Lynde Dix, it was all too real. So, how does a genteel schoolteacher end up visiting a Massachusetts prison in the first place? Call it fate, destiny, or a series of odd coincidences. Whatever it was, it sent Dix on a collision course with history.

Dix had been asked to teach a Sunday school class for women at the East Cambridge Jail. Simple enough? After all, she was a seasoned teacher, no stranger to unruly classrooms or the intricacies of the human mind. But nothing could prepare her for the horror she'd encounter in the dimly lit corners of that prison. Can you remember when something you saw didn't sit right with you, like a puzzle piece forced into the wrong spot?

The conditions were appalling. The mentally ill were lumped in with the criminals, chained to walls in unheated, unfurnished cells. If you've ever felt helpless, imagine being confined like an animal, devoid of dignity or even the most basic human comforts. Makes you shiver, doesn't it?

This was when mental illness was grossly misunderstood, stigmatized, and shamefully neglected. We're talking about an era when people believed you could 'catch' insanity or those mentally ill were possessed. Yes, really. It's like believing the Earth is flat in the age of satellite imagery.

It's said that a single moment can change the trajectory of your life. For Dix, this was it. She couldn't look away or pretend she hadn't seen the inhumanity staring her in the face. Ever felt like you had to do something because if you didn't, who would? That was Dix for you. She was a doer, not a talker. No armchair activism for this woman.

Dix didn't march out of there and straight into legislative chambers, yelling for reform. Oh, no. She knew that to fight this fight, she'd need more than just passion; she'd need irrefutable facts. Think of it as gearing up before the big battle; instead of swords and shields, her arsenal was data. She spent the next two years investigating conditions in other jails and almshouses around the state. Dix was building her case, brick by incontrovertible brick.

The Shockwaves: When Words Become Weapons

Armed with her damning evidence, Dix penned a powerful document like a cannonball fired directly at the hearts of Massachusetts legislators. She didn't mince words, and why should she? The situation was dire, demanding immediate action. If you've ever wondered if one person could make a difference, here's your answer.

Legislative Action: The First Mile in a Marathon

Now, with such a compelling report, change would come swiftly. But let's not kid ourselves; bureaucracy is seldom a sprint. It's like a slow waltz where the dancers sometimes forget the steps. However, slow progress is still progress. Her lobbying led to massive overhauls in how the mentally ill were treated in Massachusetts, setting a precedent for other states.

The Ripple Effect: When a Stone Becomes a Wave

This visit to the Massachusetts prison wasn't just a pivotal point in Dix's life; it was a seismic event that changed how America treated its most vulnerable. Can one person change the world? Maybe not the whole world, but indeed, their corner of it. And if enough corners change, you've got a revolution on your hands before you know it.

You know that phrase, "Be the change you wish to see in the world"? Dorothea Dix is the embodiment of that ideal. She didn't just witness suffering and lament it; she rolled up her sleeves and did something about it. And that, my friends, is how history is made. Dix wasn't the first to see the wretched conditions of 19th-century asylums, but she was the first to look, really look, and say, "Not on my watch."

So, what's the take-home message here? Never underestimate the power of a single visit, moment, or person to act as the catalyst for monumental change. Because sometimes, all it takes is one person to stand up and say, "Enough is enough." And let's be honest: if Dorothea Lynde Dix taught us anything, one person can make big waves.

First-Hand Accounts of Appalling Conditions

Have you ever walked into a tense room where you could cut the air with a knife? Now, imagine that pressure multiplied a hundred times. Imagine darkness so thick that it envelops your soul. That's how Dorothea Dix felt when she first peered into the gloom of the asylums and prisons she visited.

When Paper and Ink Aren't Enough

Dorothea knew she couldn't just waltz into the legislative chamber, wave her arms, and expect change. Nah, she needed something more potent. She needed to show lawmakers the gnarly, unvarnished truth in a way that they could not ignore. Think of the impact of the rawest forms of journalism you've ever seen, the ones that make your heart drop to your stomach. She aimed to bring that unfiltered reality into those musty legislative halls.

Shattered Illusions

The asylums were not like what you see in sanitized TV dramas. Forget neatly made beds and white uniforms. No, what Dix saw could've been a backdrop for Dante's Inferno. Men and women, young and old, huddled in dark corners, chained like animals and stripped of their humanity. Does it remind you of medieval dungeons? You wouldn't be far off. These were places where sanity went to die and where society's outcasts were conveniently swept under the rug.

Unforgettable Faces: The Living Evidence

Dix could have cited statistics; numbers are robust in their own right. But she chose to present case studies, accounts so personal and detailed they might as well have been short stories. Have you ever read something that made you feel like you were experiencing it for yourself? That was her aim. She wanted lawmakers to see the despair in the woman's eyes as she rocked back and forth on a barren floor. She wanted them to hear the wails echoing in corridors where no sunlight dared to venture.

The Unspoken Misery

Picture this: a man in his 30s, chained to a wall in a small, unheated cell, clothed in tattered rags that barely provide warmth. His eyes, hollow from years of torment, meet yours. At that moment, you don't see a madman but a human being. Dix painted these vivid images with her words. She wanted people to feel uncomfortable. You know that sense of awkwardness when someone talks about an issue no one wants to address?

She was tapping into that, shaking society by its shoulders and saying, "Wake up!"

The Tales That Echo Through Time

Dorothea was presenting more than just case studies. She was narrating epics, tales of sorrow and despair that could rival any Greek tragedy. Imagine telling stories so compelling that they echo through history, like the haunting resonance of a bell. That's what Dix achieved. She didn't just paint a picture; she crafted an entire gallery of human suffering, each portrait more unsettling than the last.

Fanning the Flames of Social Conscience

Let Dorothea be your lesson if you've ever felt like your small action couldn't make a dent in a monumental issue. Her first-hand accounts were like pebbles thrown into a still pond; the ripples spread far and wide. These accounts weren't just reports; they were calls to action, loud cries from the souls she encountered on her journey.

Have you ever lit a fire? At first, it's just a flicker, almost delicate. But if you feed and nurture it, that fire grows. Dorothea's accounts were the spark, the initial flicker in a blaze that would spread across the United States and beyond. It's like that quote, "A spark can start a fire that burns the entire prairie." She was that spark, and the prairie was an entire nation's ignorance and apathy.

Did it Make a Difference?

You bet it did. Dix's meticulous detailing and passionate advocacy were like a surgical strike on the fortress of public indifference. Her first-hand accounts were her most potent weapons, breaking down the walls of resistance and paving the way for an era of reform.

So the next time you wonder if one person's observations or outrage can make a difference, remember Dorothea Lynde Dix. Sometimes, all it takes is one voice to shatter the silence, one pen to rewrite the narrative, and one heart to change the course of history.

Chapter 4

The Awakening - Dix's Moral Imperative

So, you're curious how Dorothea Dix went from being an observer to an advocate. Well, let me tell you, it wasn't a light-switch moment. No, it was more of a crescendo, a slowly building drumroll that finally burst into a full-blown symphony. There's a difference between knowing something needs to be done and doing it. So, let's dig into how Dorothea transitioned from realization to action.

The realization of her mission

Dorothea Dix didn't wake up one morning with a grand plan to revolutionize the American mental health system. No, these things often unfold slowly, don't they? A series of events, encounters, and a bit of divine intervention pushed her toward her true calling. It's like a mosaic slowly coming together, each piece clicking into its destined spot. And once you see the whole picture, you can't unsee it. That's what happened to Dix. Her realization didn't happen overnight; a crescendo reached a deafening pitch, drowning out all other options and paths.

By the time she toured that prison, Dorothea had already been a teacher and had established her schools. But hold on a minute. Why would someone so enmeshed in the field of education pivot so dramatically? It's a question worth asking.

Teaching was her first love, but she had an enormous love looming—humanity itself. It was a love so vast and all-encompassing that when she saw suffering that others ignored or accepted, she couldn't turn away.

You know how we all have that voice in our minds? The one that tells us right from wrong? Most of us manage to drown it out when it becomes inconvenient. But for Dorothea, that voice became her North Star. A moral imperative that could neither be ignored nor quieted. She knew she had a mission, one much grander than herself. And guess what? She listened to that voice. Not just listen. She acted.

To pivot from teaching to advocating for the mentally ill wasn't a tiny leap; it was a monumental vault. And it took immense courage. Why? Because this was the 19th century, folks. A woman advocating for policy change? Standing before the Massachusetts legislature? Writing scathing reports about prison conditions? Come on. If that isn't audacity, I don't know what is.

But it was more than audacity. It was a recognition that her life had to serve a greater good. She had the education, the social standing, and the will to change things. And how could she not use these tools when others with far less were suffering so much? Can you imagine the burden of that realization? Yet, it was a burden she chose to carry. And in doing so, she became more than just an advocate; she became the voice for those who had none.

Dorothea Dix knew that to walk this path would be no small feat. Think about it: She was challenging an entire system, shaking up long-standing institutions, and taking on societal norms that had been unchallenged for decades. But you know what? The greater the obstacle, the more glorious the triumph, they say. And Dix was all in, come what may.

What unfolded next was a life devoted to reform, giving voice to the voiceless, and ensuring that every human being — regardless of their mental condition — was treated with the dignity they deserved. This realization of her mission was, in essence, her awakening. A transition from someone who taught children to read and write to someone who taught a nation to care.

What would you do if confronted with such a massive task? Would you step up or step aside? The thing about Dorothea Dix is that stepping aside wasn't in her DNA. No, she had to step up. For her, it was a moral imperative, a strong calling that consumed her. Thank goodness it did because the world is a better place for it.

So, the next time you hear that tiny voice urging you to do something to make a difference, take a moment to listen. Who knows? Your moral imperative might be calling, waiting for you to pick up. And wouldn't it be something if you did?

Initial Attempts at Advocacy

After visiting that Massachusetts prison, Dorothea would be chomping at the bit, suitable? Well, yes and no. She was furious, but she was also cautious. How do you even begin to dismantle a system so deeply rooted in society? But as they say, a journey of a thousand miles begins with a single step, and Dorothea took that step — albeit cautiously.

The advocacy world wasn't new to her. She'd been around the block a few times with her educational pursuits. But this was different. She was no longer in the realm of chalkboards and lesson plans; she was stepping into the lion's den of politics, social norms, and let's face it — indifference. So what did she do? She did what she knew best: research.

Dorothea became an investigator, collecting information from multiple asylums and prisons. We're talking handwritten accounts, interviews, and early data collection forms. This was detective work in a time without Google or easy access to public records. And it wasn't something she was trained for. No, siree, she was flying by the seat of her pants. Have you ever been in a situation where you have to "fake it till you make it"? Yeah, that was Dorothea Dix in the early days of her advocacy.

Armed with her newly acquired evidence, Dorothea put pen to paper. But we're not discussing a hastily written op-ed or a few passionate paragraphs. She went all out. Dorothea crafted a carefully worded document that could only be described as a 'Memorial,' a plea to the Massachusetts legislature to change the conditions of the prisons and asylums. Her words were equal parts eloquent and indicting, a skilful blend that could only come from someone with both intellectual prowess and moral clarity.

Picture this: a woman in the early 19th century, standing before an assembly of men, passionately advocating for a topic most considered unspeakable. The audacity, right? And yet, she did it. But it wasn't as if the assembly suddenly burst into applause and reformed the system overnight, far from it. There was pushback, ridicule, and even mockery. Sound familiar? It's the age-old story of change facing resistance. But Dorothea wasn't about to back down.

Instead of recoiling, she doubled down. Dix started networking, gathering allies in high places. She knew she couldn't be a lone wolf in this; systemic change requires collective effort. Have you ever felt so strongly about something that you couldn't help but draw people into your cause? Well, that was Dorothea. People listened, not just because of her compelling evidence but because her conviction was palpable. It's like trying to ignore a blazing fire in a dark room — you just can't.

This early phase of advocacy was filled with trials and tribulations. Imagine being in her shoes. You're pushing against centuries of inertia, deeply entrenched beliefs, and outright disdain for the marginalized. How do you keep going? For Dorothea, the answer was simple: she couldn't keep going. There's something to be said about the moral fibre of someone who refuses to back down in the face of impossible odds. It's like watching a single flower push through a crack in solid concrete. Against all logic, it grows.

These initial attempts at advocacy were her training ground. The lessons she learned, the allies she made, and the obstacles she overcame all shaped her into the powerhouse advocate she would later become. Like an athlete in the early mornings before sunrise, she was conditioning herself for the marathon. And trust me, it was a marathon.

So there you have it—the birth of an advocate. A trial by fire, if you will. But hey, as the saying goes, "Smooth seas do not make skillful sailors." Dorothea Dix's early advocacy might not have changed the world overnight. Still, it set the stage for the monumental changes to come. And if that's not an awakening, I don't know what is.

Chapter 5

The Battlefront - Lobbying the Legislatures

Sometimes in life, a person's got to do more than talk the talk. They've got to walk the walk, you know? And when it came to Dorothea Dix, walking wasn't enough; she practically sprinted. We've touched on how she took her cause to the Massachusetts Legislature with her "Memorial," but that was just the tip of the iceberg. The part we rarely hear about? The relentless power of her reports. If you imagine boring stacks of paper filled with legalese, think again. Let's get into the nitty-gritty!

Her Memorial to the Massachusetts Legislature

Imagine pouring your heart and soul into a piece of writing, knowing full well that it might be the catalyst for monumental change — or a flop heard around the state. That was Dorothea's "Memorial," her impassioned plea to the Massachusetts Legislature.

What's in a name, you ask? In the case of Dix's "Memorial," it's a call to remember the forgotten, the incarcerated, the mentally ill — those whom society would rather sweep under the rug. A "memorial" conjures up images of monuments and remembrance. Clever, right? Dix wasn't just lobbying for reform; she advocated for societal memory and collective conscience.

How'd she go about it? Well, she didn't mince words. Dorothea described the conditions she witnessed in vivid detail, as though painting a gruesome portrait with her words. But it wasn't sensationalist or exploitative; it was a hard-hitting reality check. How do you make a room full of politicians listen? You shove the truth down their throats until they can't look away.

Let's not sugarcoat it: Dix was taking a gamble. Speaking in political circles, women in the 19th century were often ridiculed or ignored. Even being there was a radical act. What was it like, do you think, standing in a hall designed by men, for men, to advocate for those whom even men considered unworthy of advocacy?

You're probably wondering, did her "Memorial" do the trick? Short answer: Kinda, sort of. Change is never instantaneous, especially when challenging deep-seated prejudices and a bureaucratic nightmare. But her efforts were worthwhile. Dix's Memorial rattled some cages and unsettled some comfy armchairs in the legislative chambers.

The result? Well, let's say they didn't throw her out. Lawmakers started talking, and when politicians talk, things happen—slowly, yes, but inevitably. Committees were formed, reports were filed, and bills were even drafted. But it wasn't as if her "Memorial" magically fixed everything. Heck, no! The lawmakers dilly-dallied, made excuses, and threw up roadblocks. Remember, this is the legislature we're talking about: a labyrinthine hall of mirrors where progress can get lost wandering for years.

In some ways, her "Memorial" was less of an endpoint and more of a starting gun. Dix had laid down the gauntlet, and there was no turning back. If she were a sprinter, this would be the moment she exploded off the starting blocks, muscles coiled like springs, eyes dead set on the finish line.

Dorothea knew she had to keep the pressure up, and boy, did she. She followed her "Memorial" with more visits, meetings, and speeches. Think about it: How often have you gotten a 'maybe' and felt disheartened? Not Dix. A 'maybe' to her was an opening, a foot in the door, a chink in the armour. And she was more than willing to turn that 'maybe' into a 'yes.'

For anyone else, the convoluted world of 19th-century politics could have been a vortex of despair. But Dorothea Dix was made of sterner stuff. Whether you call it resilience, tenacity, or downright stubbornness, Dix had it in spades. She became a frequent figure in the legislative corridors. This presence couldn't be ignored, like a persistent drumbeat in the background score of a revolution. And all of this started with one document — her Memorial to the Massachusetts Legislature.

In the grand tapestry of social reform, the threads of political lobbying are often tangled, messy, and frustratingly slow to weave. But they're crucial. Dix's Memorial was one such golden thread, an initial stitch in a much larger pattern of change. The immediate impact? Not earth-shattering. But the ripples? They would eventually turn into waves, crashing against the shores of apathy and indifference.

So, the next time you think of Dorothea Dix, don't just picture her as the compassionate caregiver or the keen observer. Imagine her as a lobbyist, a political tactician, a woman who walked into the lion's den and roared louder than all of them. After all, isn't that what heroes do? They fight battles on fronts most of us don't even realize exist. Dix was no exception. She epitomized what happens when moral clarity meets political savvy — a force to be reckoned with. And that, my friends, is the essence of her battlefront: the Massachusetts Legislature.

The Persuasive Power of Her Reports

When you think of persuasive writing, what comes to mind? A smooth-talking salesman or a politician's speech? Well, Dix's reports were different from those. They were explosive charges of truth, detonated in the chambers of power. What made them so impactful? Glad you asked.

You've heard the saying, "The pen is mightier than the sword," right? The pen was her weapon of choice for Dorothea Dix, and she wielded it like a skilled duelist. It wasn't just the facts she presented but how she presented them. Think about it: How do you make a pile of statistics and observations shake people to their very core? You drape them in the human experience. That's precisely what Dix did.

Picture a dark room filled with officials, comfortable in their seats, fumbling through papers, and — wham! — in comes

Dorothea Dix with her reports. Let's get this straight: These weren't just documents; they were narratives, stories, and character arcs, complete with villains and heroes. It was as if Dickens had penned investigative journalism. What do you suppose that does to a lawmaker who's used to skimming dry, bullet-pointed reports? It knocks the wind right out of them.

And it wasn't just the legislators who were moved. The public read her reports, too. In a democracy, the Court of Public Opinion has its kind of power. Why? Because politicians, for all their quirks and follies, listen when their constituents raise a ruckus. Dix's reports became talking points at dinner tables, taverns, and social circles. Her writing broke out of the stale atmosphere of government chambers. It started popping up in the conversations of everyday folks. And when that happens — boy oh boy — you've got yourself a revolution.

Now, what was in these reports? They were filled with firsthand accounts from the hellholes they called "asylums." And the term 'asylum' — doesn't it just make you shudder? You hear it and think of sanctuary, refuge, and safety. But what Dix exposed was nothing short of a horror show. Caged like animals, the patients she described were often naked, starving, and chained to walls. Her accounts weren't just recounting; they were an indictment of a society that had lost its moral compass. And believe me, people listened. How could you not?

Did her reports immediately flip the switch? Did asylums across the nation transform overnight? Well, no, that's not how change works. But what it did do was initiate a long overdue conversation. You see, the first step to solving a problem is admitting there's one. Dix's reports didn't just drop that truth bomb—they ensured everyone heard the explosion.

And remember, the battle she was fighting was against a flawed system but also deep-seated prejudices. Just getting legislators to read her reports was a feat in itself. Women of her time were expected to be seen and not heard. Well, Dorothea Dix refused to be invisible. She was seen, listened to, and, most importantly, acted upon.

Imagine lighting a match in a dark room. That's what Dix did with her reports. They were that first flicker of light, highlighting the corners filled with society's neglect and shame. They initiated a chain reaction. Investigations were launched, reforms were discussed, and, bit by bit, the needle started to move. You might not win the war with a single battle, but you can turn the tide.

So, the next time you think about Dorothea Dix, remember her as a social reformer and a master communicator. A woman who knew the worth of words and used them to wage a war against apathy and ignorance. What's that old saying again? Ah, yes, "Words are, in my not-so-humble opinion, our most inexhaustible source of magic." Dix knew this magic well, and she used it to unlock doors that had been bolted shut for far too long. So, yeah, Dorothea Dix? She was more than just a reformer; she was a warrior with a pen, a lobbyist with a heart, and a wordsmith with a soul.

Chapter 6

Victory & Vexation - Policy Triumphs And Obstacles

Isn't life a roller coaster? One minute, you're on cloud nine, feeling invincible, and the next, you're plummeting into despair. Now imagine the highs and lows of trying to change society's views on mental health in the 1800s. You're thinking it sounds like a Herculean task. Well, that was Dorothea Dix's reality. The road to reform isn't a straight path — it's filled with thrilling victories and heart-wrenching setbacks.

Successes in Law Reform

Have you ever seen those old black-and-white movies where the protagonist makes this grand, passionate speech, and just like that, everything magically changes? Well, spoiler alert: Real life's not like that. Dix had her movie-moment speeches, but it took so much more than eloquent words to make a dent in the system.

Remember that report we talked about earlier? The one that stunned legislators with its vivid depictions of the horrors faced by the mentally ill? Sure, it was a pivotal point, but do you think one report was enough to sway an entire legislative body? If you guessed "no", you'd be right.

But here's where things get interesting. Whenever Dix presented her findings, she did so with such unwavering conviction that she started gaining allies in high places. And let me tell you something: when you're battling the Goliath that is the established norm, having a few Davids by your side can make all the difference. Dix's voice grew louder with each legislative session, echoed by those who had come to see the truth in her words.

Now, picture this: The Massachusetts State Legislature, 1843. Dorothea Dix stands confidently, reports in hand, surrounded by allies. And here, she experienced one of her first significant policy victories — the bill for expanded mental health facilities in Massachusetts. Was it an easy win? Heck, 'no'. But was it worth it? A resounding 'yes'.

The ripple effect was astounding. Her success in Massachusetts paved the way for similar legislation in Rhode Island and New Jersey. By the 1850s, more than a dozen states had seen significant reforms in their mental health policies — all thanks to Dix and her band of allies.

Remember the story of the little engine that could? "I think I can, I think I can." Dix was that engine, but she didn't think she could; she knew she could. And she did. But like every story with peaks, there were inevitable valleys.

With every success came detractors—those who resisted change or felt threatened. It's human nature, I guess. Change can be terrifying when you've been doing something a certain way for so long, even if it's wrong. Dix faced her share of opposition, from politicians with vested interests in maintaining the status quo to private asylum owners who saw her reforms as a direct threat to their income.

So yes, Dorothea Dix's journey wasn't all sunshine and rainbows. It was a constant ebb and flow of triumphs and tribulations. But you know what's remarkable? Through it all, she never lost sight of her goal. Every setback only served to fuel her fire, pushing her to work harder, advocate louder, and shine a spotlight on the darkness that many wished to keep hidden.

In the grand tapestry of Dorothea Dix's life, her successes in law reform are but a few threads — albeit vibrant, shimmering ones. They testify to what one determined individual can achieve with persistence, passion, and a little stubbornness. So, channel a little bit of Dorothea Dix the next time you face an uphill battle. After all, if she could change the world in petticoats and a bonnet, just think of what you could do in your sneakers.

The Naysayers in the Halls of Power

Have you ever walked into a room and felt you didn't belong? Now imagine that room is filled with high-ranking officials, lawmakers, and men — yes, mostly men — who control the fate of your passionate cause. Sounds intimidating, right? That was Dix's playground. A woman in a man's world pushes an agenda that many consider too radical and forward-thinking.

When she stepped up to the podium with her research, her eyes were often met with disdain or mockery from legislators.

Her meticulous reports and impassioned pleas could often fall on deaf ears. Why? It could be because ignoring a problem is more straightforward than solving it. Maybe because some people don't change, no matter how much you want them to.

The Financial Roadblocks

Picture this — you've made the most persuasive argument ever, you've even got lawmakers nodding in agreement, and when you think you're close to victory, someone asks, "But how do we pay for it?" Boom! Suddenly, the momentum halts, and the room turns cold. Financial constraints were a significant roadblock for Dix. Legislators would hem and haw over budgets, appropriations, and allocations. Many of her proposed bills were scrapped or heavily altered due to the 'almighty dollar.'

The Infighting Among Allies

Surprisingly, not all the opposition came from her detractors. Even those ostensibly on the same side of the issue had their own ideas about how to bring about change. It's like when you're on a team project — everyone wants a good grade, but no one can agree on how to get it. The infighting among reformers sometimes led to diluted initiatives, reduced funding, or failed legislative efforts.

The Shifting Public Opinion

Have you ever noticed how public opinion is like the wind? One moment, it's at your back, pushing you forward, and the next, it's in your face, trying to hold you back. The public's attitude towards mental health was often fickle, influenced by stigmas, myths, and plain old ignorance. Dix had to fight the system and the prevailing public opinion that often stigmatized the mentally ill as "lunatics" or "hopeless cases."

The Personal Toll: A Battle Within

Let's remember that Dix was human, not a superhero. The endless battles, political manoeuvring, and disappointments took a toll on her. Physically and emotionally, the stress manifested in various ailments. Dix often fell ill and was occasionally bedridden, but guess what? She never quit. She embodied the phrase, "When the going gets tough, the tough get going."

So, what do we make of all these challenges and setbacks? Did they slow her down? Yes. Did they stop her? Absolutely not. Dix's story is not a fairy tale; it's better because it's real. It's about not giving up, even when the world gives you a million reasons to. It's about being the lone voice in the wilderness until the wilderness listens and joins your chorus.

In facing and overcoming these obstacles, Dix didn't just build sandcastles at the tide's edge; she laid down bricks and mortar, constructing a legacy that would withstand the test of time—and tides. And in that resilience, she taught us all a lesson in courage that we could all stand to learn.

The Triumph in Frustration: A Shifting Landscape

What happens when life gives you lemons? The old saying suggests making lemonade, but Dix was beyond that — she was making lemon meringue pie, complete with a flaky crust of legal reform and a filling of improved mental healthcare. Sure, not every venture was a resounding success. Still, every setback had its silver lining, an unintended consequence that often turned the tables in her favour.

Why? Because each obstacle she encountered forced Dix to innovate. Faced with financial roadblocks? She became a master of grassroots fundraising, uniting local communities behind her cause. When lawmakers rejected her proposals? Dix refined her approach, adopting a more nuanced, tactical angle.

Persistence Amidst Discouragement: A Lesson for Us All

Have you ever had one of those days? You know, the ones where everything goes wrong, and you just want to throw in the towel? Dix had years like that. Yet, she never quit. The word 'quit' wasn't in her vocabulary. Why? Because the mission, the change she was fighting for, was more significant than any obstacle or setback.

When Dix's initial reports were met with derision or fell upon deaf ears, she could have retreated, discouraged and defeated. But she didn't. Instead, she dug in her heels, conducted more research, and came back swinging with even more compelling arguments. Each roadblock led to a detour that enriched her journey and reinforced her resolve.

Dix's Tactical Evolution: Turning Obstacles into Opportunities

Whoever said, "What doesn't kill you makes you stronger," might have been discussing Dorothea Dix. Each obstacle she faced taught her something valuable about the battlefield she navigated. With every 'no,' she found a new way to argue for a 'yes.'

The persuasive power of her reports didn't just come from the facts she presented but also from how she presented them. Over time, she learned to speak the language of the legislators — crafting her arguments regarding economics, public safety, and even national pride.

And let's remember Dix also capitalized on the change in public opinion. Yes, the wind of public sentiment is fickle, but if you can learn to harness it, you can soar. As mental health started gaining more recognition, thanks partly to her efforts, Dix rode that wave of change to achieve some of her most significant policy victories.

The Never-ending Battle: Dix's Legacy in the Face of Struggle

Even though Dorothea Dix has long left this world, the battle she fought is far from over. But here's the thing — every time a new mental health reform bill is passed, patients receive the care they deserve. Whenever we chip away at the societal stigma surrounding mental health, Dix scores another posthumous victory. Her legacy, built in the face of overwhelming obstacles, lives on. And you know what? That's what you call a win in my book.

Dix's story of confronting challenges head-on is an inspiration. Her life reminds us that when you're fighting for something that matters, opposition isn't just expected; it's a sign you're on the right track. Because if you're not ruffling feathers, you're probably not flying.

The Weight of Controversy: The Dix-Hamlin Bill

Have you ever been so close to something you've worked tirelessly for, only to see it slip through your fingers? This was a bitter pill Dix had to swallow with the failure of the Dix-Hamlin Bill, aimed at setting aside federal land to fund asylums for the mentally ill.

What went wrong? It passed both houses of Congress, a triumph considering the divisive political atmosphere. But in an almost Shakespearean twist, President Franklin Pierce vetoed it. A crushing setback? Absolutely. But it was also a stark reminder that no victory comes without its share of defeat.

A Global Impact: The Transatlantic Journey

Remember when you took a leap of faith, stepping out of your comfort zone? Dix did just that but on an international scale. Her work was more comprehensive than the U.S. shores. No, she took her campaign overseas, influencing European mental health reform.

Why does this matter? Because advocacy isn't a local issue; it's a human issue. Dix's efforts across the Atlantic proved that her mission had global resonance, a message that transcended borders and cultures. She faced new challenges — different political systems, social stigmas, and languages Still, Dix navigated these obstacles with the same determination that had fueled her American campaigns.

The Final Act: Life After Advocacy

What do you do when you've devoted your life to a cause? For Dix, the answer was simple: keep going. Her later years were not a period of rest or retreat but a continuation of her lifelong mission, now channelled into serving as Superintendent of Army Nurses during the Civil War.

Picture this: The woman who had fought so hard for mental health reform was now in the midst of a war, tending to the wounded and afflicted. It wasn't a glamorous job, but it was essential. And Dix was no stranger to rolling up her sleeves and doing the necessary work, no matter how challenging.

The Inheritance We Carry: Dix's Legacy in Modern Times

So here we are, years after Dix's death, still talking about her, still inspired by her. What does that tell you? It tells you that true legacies are built on courage, resilience, and an unwavering commitment to improving the world.

Dix's story is more than a historical footnote; it's a blueprint for effective advocacy. It's a lesson in how one person's unwavering commitment can ignite change, even when faced with insurmountable obstacles. And it leaves us with a question: What will we struggle for? What will be our legacy?

You see, Dix's life wasn't just about her; it's also about us. It's about the choices we make, the battles we choose, and the legacies we leave. It poses the ultimate rhetorical question: If Dorothea Dix could overcome her era's formidable challenges to champion humanity, what's stopping us?

And so, Dorothea Dix's life story ends. However, the narrative she started is still being written—by policymakers, mental health advocates, and perhaps, by you.

Chapter 7

Expanding Horizons - Beyond America's Borders

Suppose you've wondered how deeply a single individual's influence can penetrate. In that case, the story of Dorothea Lynde Dix should be your primer. She's often celebrated as an American hero, but did you know her impact rippled across the pond and into European history? Yeah, her legacy is quite the globe-trotter!

Let's take a step back. What was European mental health care like before Dix began on European soil? Remember the days of dial-up internet? Slow, frustrating, unreliable? That's what mental health care felt like in many European nations. England, Scotland, France, and Italy had their own versions of "care," but much of it was medieval at best. Patients were mistreated, misunderstood, and miserably supported.

A Flicker in the Darkness: Dix's Arrival

You know that feeling when you light a candle in a dark room? How suddenly everything looks different, more hopeful? That's precisely the feeling Dix brought with her. When she first toured European asylums and institutions, she wasn't there as a mere spectator. No, Dix had her sleeves rolled up from day one, ready to kindle that flicker into a flame. But how did she do it?

Actions Speak Louder: Unveiling the Problems

Dorothea Dix had a gift, one that went beyond mere advocacy. She could paint a vivid picture with her words, make you feel the walls closing in on you as she described the cramped asylums, and make you squirm at the detailing of shackles and chains. And she unleashed this power of description in her meticulous reports and memorials. Why? To bring about an undeniable awareness, an unavoidable urge to act among the European elite. And boy, did she succeed.

The Power of Ink: Turning Words into Laws

Dix was no armchair activist; she knew words had to lead to action. In countries like Scotland, France, and Italy, she didn't just point out the problems — she offered solutions, sometimes even drafting legislation herself. Can you imagine that? An American woman influencing European laws in the 19th century! It's like a culinary amateur suggesting a new recipe to a Michelin-starred chef and adding it to the menu.

Her impact on European mental health care reform

Would you believe that Dix's involvement led to law reforms, institutional restructuring, and a paradigm shift in how Europe viewed mental health? You better. The "Dix effect," as some would call it, cascaded across nations. England saw transformations in their Lunacy Laws, Scotland revamped their asylum conditions, and Italy initiated widespread reforms. Her influence was such that she became an unofficial but highly respected transatlantic ambassador for mental health care reform.

But you know what's the hardest thing to change? It's not the laws or institutions; it's people's minds. And Dix had an uncanny knack for this. She didn't just convince lawmakers; she swayed public opinion. With her articulate reports and public speeches, she planted seeds of empathy and understanding within societies traditionally steeped in stigma and ignorance.

Isn't it incredible how a single individual can spark a revolution of thought and policy across diverse cultures and nations? Dorothea Dix wasn't just an American icon but a global symbol of compassion, courage, and change. Sure, her roots were on American soil, but what was her impact? That was universal. It's like she turned the world into her canvas, each brush stroke aimed at erasing the grim past and painting a brighter, more humane future.

When Worlds Collide: Comparing Dix's Influence at Home and Abroad

Let's be honest here—Dorothea Lynde Dix was no ordinary American woman of her time. Her influence spanned continents, and her impact reached corners of the world that most Americans of her era could only imagine. But how does her impact on mental health care reform in Europe stack up against her work in America? To answer that, we've got to do a bit of time travel and look at the landscapes she was dealing with in both places.

The American Battleground: Where It All Began

Picture a young America, still green behind the ears, attempting to figure out how to care for the mentally ill. We're talking about a place where asylums more closely resembled dungeons and where the term 'care' was employed loosely. Dix found her calling here, diving headlong into this American abyss of neglect. Her first strides, such as the landmark Memorial to the Massachusetts Legislature, sparked a fire that would spread like wildfire across the States.

Crossing The Pond: Europe's Staleness Craves Change

On the other side of the Atlantic, Europe was already an old continent with centuries-long traditions, for better or worse. Their asylums? Just as deplorable, if not worse, despite being ensconced in cultures that prided themselves on civilization and enlightenment. Dix, ever the adaptable warrior, didn't charge in blindly; she modified her strategies to fit the different cultural contexts. Her approach had to be more than a copy-paste job from her American playbook.

Grassroots vs. Aristocrats: Audience Matters, Folks!

In America, Dix had the luxury of a democratic system — a "power to the people" situation. Her passionate pleas and detailed reports could touch the hearts of the masses and politicians alike. But Europe? She had to knock on the gilded doors of aristocrats, scholars, and even royals. How do you convince a count or a duke that the way they've been doing things for centuries is just plain wrong?

Dix rose to the challenge, realizing she had to change her pitch without losing her core message. Once channelled through legislative halls in America, the power of her words found a new stage in private parlours and royal chambers in Europe. A woman of many talents, indeed.

Policy Shifts: The American Domino Effect vs. The European Tapestry

Remember that scene in a movie where the protagonist pushes a single domino, and it sets off a chain reaction? That's an excellent way to visualize what Dix did in America. Her first legislative victories created a momentum that other states found hard to resist.

In Europe, however, it was more like weaving a complex tapestry. Each thread had to be carefully inserted, considering the existing patterns. Here, change was incremental, each victory hard-fought. There were only a few templates that could be applied everywhere. Each country required a tailored approach, and Dix provided just that with her incredible adaptability.

So, who got the better deal—America or Europe? It's a tough call. In America, Dix's efforts led to systemic change that set new standards. In Europe, her influence was less uniform but still groundbreaking. She penetrated age-old traditions and catalyzed reforms that many thought were impossible.

The beauty of it all? She was one woman fighting the same fight on two very different fronts. On American soil, her work laid the foundation for the mental health system we're still improving today. In Europe, her influence served as a catalyst for change, shaking up long-standing institutions and beliefs. She was a force of nature that refused to be ignored in both arenas.

Can you imagine being a fly on the wall during one of her impassioned speeches? To hear her take on two different worlds, dissect their flaws, and offer tangible solutions would have been awe-inspiring. In a time when the sound of a woman's voice was often drowned out, Dorothea Dix's words echoed loud and clear on both sides of the Atlantic.

Chapter 8

The Collaborators - Friends And Foes

We all know the saying, "It takes a village." And let me tell you, reforming an entire mental health care system was not a job for the faint-hearted or lone wolves. Dorothea Dix had a village of like-minded individuals, each with a role in the broader narrative.

The Harmony of Dix and Samuel Gridley Howe

Samuel Gridley Howe, the guy renowned for his work on education for the blind, was someone you could call Dix's co-warrior in the battle for reform. These two weren't just casual associates; they shared a friendship grounded in mutual respect and vision. Think of them as a dynamic duo, both fierce advocates in their own right and an unstoppable force.

Howe understood the balance between idealism and practicality, much like Dix herself. In a time when those with disabilities were sidelined and stigmatized, Howe was fighting his own battle, parallel to Dix's, for better care and education for the visually impaired. Their missions intersected in many ways, from advocacy to political lobbying. Could you imagine their dinner conversations? Likely a blend of strategy, deep intellectual discussion, and, of course, the optimistic hope for a better future.

The Intellectual Symbiosis with Horace Mann

Then there's Horace Mann, another juggernaut in the reform world. An advocate for educational reform, Mann and Dix were birds of a feather. Dix's push for better mental health treatment had a classroom counterpart in Mann's passion for improving public education. While Mann fought for the chalkboard, Dix battled for the asylum, but both were warriors for human dignity.

They'd share insights, brainstorm, critique, and argue to be a fly on the wall during one of their intense debates! But they'd always return to their united front because their end goals were essentially the same: a more humane, enlightened society.

Diverging Visions: Where Allies Become Adversaries

However, only some people who start as an ally remain one. Even with her closest collaborators, Dix had her share of political and philosophical disagreements. Whether it was over funding mechanisms, state vs. federal jurisdiction, or the role of religion in care, tension was never too far away.

In some ways, this was inevitable. You put a group of passionate reformers in a room, and while the goal may be the same, the pathways could be vastly different. The trick is to navigate these disagreements without tearing the whole ship apart.

Partners in Progress or Obstacles in Disguise?

What about those who started as foes but aided Dix's mission? It's a funny thing, isn't it? Sometimes, your most vocal critics can provide the resistance that refines your ideas. Dix encountered skepticism from medical professionals, politicians, and even the public. But instead of dismissing these detractors, she listened, adapted, and often won them over.

Some of her most effective strategies were born from the crucible of opposition. Whether they intended to or not, these foes helped shape Dix's mission into a more resilient, compelling force. After all, even steel needs to go through fire to get its strength, right?

The Ties that Bind: Unity and Division

By the end of her career, Dix had built a network of collaborators that was as varied as influential. It was a challenging ride, but then again, revolution seldom is. As she knew, change is neither easy nor the work of one. You can have all the vision in the world, but you need hands to help you build it.

Dorothea Dix did not act alone, and that's not a point against her; it's a testament to her ability to lead, collaborate, and adapt. Whether it was Howe's supportive friendship or Mann's educational zest, each person contributed something unique to her mission, even if they didn't always see eye to eye.

Dorothea Dix is undoubtedly a bold and defining thread in the grand tapestry of social reform. But look closer, and you'll see she's interwoven with others — friends and foes alike — each contributing to a larger, more intricate, and more beautiful design. Would she have been as effective without them? It's a question worth pondering. However, one thing is clear: her story isn't just about a lone woman's fight but the collective struggle for human dignity.

The Web of Political Alliances: Congress and Beyond

Let's talk politics for a minute. Dix wasn't just cozying up to fellow reformers; she was also putting in the legwork on Capitol Hill. You may think this lobbying is for slick politicians and businessmen, but you'd be wrong. Dix was at home in the marble halls of Congress as she was in the asylums and hospitals she toured.

Why? Because if you're looking to change the world — or at least a good slice of America — you have to aim for the top. Dix knew she couldn't act as a lone wolf; she needed legislative muscle. Friends in high places? Dix had them. Foes, too. Each played a part in the drama of Dix's reformist journey. Sure, she was disappointed — heartbroken, even — when bills she backed failed to pass. But did she throw in the towel? No way. If anything, the setbacks only fueled her fire.

Working Across Party Lines: A Lesson for Today?

What's striking is how Dix garnered bipartisan support for her causes. In a political climate where the division was as American as apple pie, Dix somehow cut through the noise. You see, suffering doesn't care about your party affiliation; it's an equal-opportunity burden. So, for Dix, why should the solutions be any different?

She had the ear of Whigs and Democrats alike, convincing folks on both sides that improving mental health care was not just humane—it was American. No small feat in a divided Congress. How did she do it? Well, let's just say Dix knew how to speak the language of empathy as fluently as she did the language of policy.

The Landscape of Resistance: From Skepticism to Outright Hostility

Of course, it wasn't all rosy. Dix faced her share of naysayers inside and outside the political sphere. Some thought her a naïve woman out of her depth. Others found her insistence on humane treatment for the mentally ill a drain on public resources. Remember, this was an era where some still believed mental illness resulted from moral failure or divine punishment.

But here's the thing: Dix wouldn't be silenced. She transformed every criticism into a stepping stone, every obstacle into an opportunity to refine her arguments. Could it be that her harshest critics were, in fact, her best teachers? The answer lies in her success, for you can only reach the mountaintop by first traversing the valley.

The Legacy of Collaboration: A Mosaic of Reform

When the curtains closed on Dix's active career, she left behind more than just a list of accomplishments. She left a legacy — a constellation of lives changed, laws enacted, and institutions reformed. She may have been the star at the center, but she didn't shine alone. Samuel Gridley Howe, Horace Mann, and congressmen of every stripe were all part of the celestial dance of change.

Each person's role, whether big or small, contentious or complementary, added a layer to Dix's life's work. They were more than just names in a story; they contributed to a shared vision of what America could be. A nation where the marginalized were seen. Where the forgotten were remembered. Where the suffering was soothed. And in today's world, where division often overshadows unity, Dix's story reminds us that meaningful change is not just an individual's work but a symphony of many.

It's a lesson we would do well to remember, wouldn't you agree? Because the push for a better world is far from over, and we all have parts yet to play. After all, a single thread is easily broken, but a tapestry — rich with many contributions — is solid and enduring. That was the truth Dorothea Dix lived by. And it's a truth worth carrying forward.

The Tangled Web of Allies and Adversaries

Have you ever tried to navigate a complex maze without a guide or a map? That's how Dorothea Dix felt as she waded through the murky waters of 19th-century American politics and social reform. You see, it takes more than courage and conviction to effect change on a monumental scale. It requires allies. But not all allies are created equal. And let's not forget about the foes — those who are quick to dismiss, undermine, or oppose you at every turn. What's fascinating about Dix's story is how she managed both. Intrigued? Let's dive in.

The Unlikely Band of Crusaders: Samuel Gridley Howe and Horace Mann

Remember those high school projects where you had to team up with classmates you hardly knew or liked? Well, imagine that, but on a life-altering, society-changing scale. Samuel Gridley Howe and Horace Mann were two such 'classmates' in Dix's life.

Howe, a doctor and abolitionist, focused on the visually impaired. Mann, an educational reformer, was the man we thank for what we now know as the American public school system. Odd bedfellows for Dix, one might think, but you'd be wrong. Why? Because when it comes to dismantling societal ills, the more, the merrier. United by a common goal — making America a better, more humane place — they lent each other credibility. They opened doors that were otherwise bolted shut. Were there disagreements? Sure. Clashes of ego? Absolutely. But when the chips were down, they banded together. The question is, could Dix have made the strides she did without them? It's doubtful.

The Political Chessboard: Navigating Friendships and Rivalries in High Places

When you're in the business of societal reform, the line between friend and foe could be more precise. That's politics for you—a delicate dance on a tightrope of ego and ambition. Dix knew this better than anyone.

Take her dealings with Congress, for instance. More was needed for a cause; you needed backers, the political heavyweights. And boy, did she get them. Senators and House members championed her bills, pushing for the creating of state psychiatric hospitals and better treatment for the mentally ill. A win, right? Not so fast. Enter the foes, stage right. Some politicians saw Dix's bills as budget sinkholes, impractical fantasies. Now, these were not mere differences of opinion but battles for the soul of America's conscience.

When Friendships Turn Sour: The Double-Edged Sword of Alliance

Have you ever had a friend who turned out to be a thorn in your side? Welcome to the world of alliances, where today's friend can become tomorrow's adversary. Dix learned this lesson the hard way. Even among her closest allies, disagreements arose — about money, methods, and the minutiae of institutional reform. These rifts sometimes splintered alliances, causing personal and public setbacks.

But here's the kicker: In the fight for justice, you learn more from your setbacks than your victories. Dix took these bumps in stride, recalibrated, and returned to the fray, her resolve fortified. Sometimes, old allies became new again, and past disagreements turned into future collaborations. A twist in the tale.

The Grand Tapestry: A Collective Quest for Reform

Let's pull back for a second and look at the bigger picture. Dix's life was a grand tapestry woven from threads of friendship, enmity, alliance, and opposition. Each person and relationship added a unique colour and texture to her mission. While we often celebrate individual heroes, it's crucial to remember that no one acts alone.

Conflicts and alliances

Conflicts and alliances are the warp and weft of any good story and, more importantly, any social reform. The yin and yang of Dix's mission were her relationships. These interactions didn't just shape her journey; they were the journey. Through the maze of friendships and foes, Dix found her way, showing us that the path to change, though fraught with challenges, is never lonely.

Have you ever wondered what a single thread can do in a vast tapestry? Maybe not much on its own, but weave it in with others, and it becomes part of something much more significant, something transformative. Dix was a master weaver in the tapestry of American social reform. Her story teaches us that, to make a difference, we must be willing to navigate the complex web of human relationships — just as she did.

Chapter 9

The Civil War Years - Dix As Superintendent Of Army Nurses

Civil War - the cataclysm that ripped America apart. You might wonder: What was a woman who'd dedicated her life to the mentally ill doing in the middle of the most violent conflict America had yet seen? Good question. The simple answer is Dorothea Dix wasn't one to sit idly by. Not when there were lives to be saved and wrongs to be righted. And so, she found herself a new frontline — the medical tents and makeshift hospitals of the Union Army. Intrigued yet? Let's dig in.

Her role in the Union Army

Picture this: Hundreds of injured soldiers moaning in pain and not nearly enough nurses to go around. A chaotic mess, right? Into this storm walks Dix. The same woman who'd kicked open the doors of asylums now aimed to reshape wartime nursing. No small feat, let me tell you. But if anyone could do it, it was Dix. The woman had a spine of steel. When the Union Army needed someone to supervise its nursing corps, they didn't have to look far. Dix was appointed Superintendent of Army Nurses, a position she took up without a salary, mind you. Imagine that: shaping the future of medical care in wartime and not earning a dime from it. That's dedication.

The General in Skirts: Facing Challenges Head-On

"War is hell," they say, but running a nursing corps in that hell? That's another level of inferno. Dix faced shortages—of supplies, trained personnel, and practically everything. And let's not forget the male medical officers who couldn't stomach the idea of a woman in charge. Remember, this was the 19th century when women were often seen but not heard. Dix, however, was neither to be seen nor dismissed. She set stringent standards for who could be a nurse: Women over 30, plain-looking, and willing to forsake fashion for functionality. Severe? Maybe. Effective? Definitely. These guidelines helped ensure that her nurses were there for one reason: to save lives. But rules alone couldn't quell resentment and resistance. How did she cope? Through sheer force of will and a boatload of tenacity, traits that had served her well in asylums and state legislatures.

A Tumultuous Tenure: What Happens When An Unstoppable Force Meets Immovable Objects?

Have you ever had a job where every step forward was met with two steps back? That's how it must've been for Dix. There were obstacles at every turn, some from the enemy, but many from within her own ranks. Disagreements with other officials, notably the quartermaster general Montgomery C. Meigs, led to frustrating roadblocks. The bureaucracy could have choked a lesser person, but not Dix. Sure, she had her moments of vexation — who wouldn't? — but she soldiered on. No pun intended.

Dix's Legacy: Not Just a Caregiver, but a Trailblazer

As the war concluded, Dix's role as Superintendent did, too. But she left an indelible mark, setting the stage for professional nursing and proving, yet again, that a determined woman could play in the big leagues, even if that league was as gritty and gruesome as war. Her insistence on discipline and training in the nursing corps transformed it from an ad hoc assemblage into an effective force, which laid the groundwork for modern nursing as we know it.

So, let's get real for a second. Was Dix a saint? No. Was she without fault or failure? Absolutely not. But what makes her exceptional is how she thrived in adversity, leaving her mark on every battle she fought, whether in asylums or army tents. Her legacy isn't just in the institutions she improved but in the innumerable lives she touched and bettered. Makes you wonder, doesn't it? What battles are you fighting, and what legacy will you leave? Dix shows us that sometimes, the most formidable warriors are those who fight not with weapons but with words, will, and an unwavering belief in the dignity of all human beings.

Dodging Bullets, Wrestling Red Tape: The Challenges of Her Role

Okay, folks, let's roll up our sleeves and get down to brass tacks. Picture this: Dorothea Dix, a woman who could convince an elephant to climb a tree if it served a noble cause. She's Superintendent of Army Nurses now. That's right — she's coordinating the women patching up wounded soldiers, running things like a general. Well, she wasn't called 'Dragon

Dix' for nothing. But boy, did she face challenges. Who wouldn't amid America's most divisive war?

Challenges, you ask? Take, for example, a military bureaucracy that moved with the speed of molasses in January. Resources were as scarce as hen's teeth — like bandages, medicines, and beds. Sounds harsh, right? It gets tougher. Dix had to manage these limited resources while navigating an ocean of red tape, sometimes having to 'borrow' supplies to keep operations afloat. Resourceful? You betcha. But oh, what a tangled web the bureaucracy wove.

If you think handling material shortages was a hurdle, imagine locking horns with high-ranking military officers who thought women had as much business managing army affairs as a cat has in a swimming pool. Yeah, that was the kind of uphill battle she faced. No matter her iron will or indomitable spirit, her every decision seemed second-guessed and scrutinized by the powers. Could you imagine having your every move watched like a hawk by folks who'd thought you weren't there in the first place? Not fun.

The Costume Drama: Her Strict Requirements for Nurses

Ah, here comes the juicy part — controversy. And this isn't your garden-variety squabble; it's a full-blown uproar. Remember, Dix had rules. Oh, did she have rules? Nurses under her charge had to be older than 30 and, let's just say, not precisely runway-ready. No jewellery, hoop skirts, and — brace yourself — no young men hanging around. Think Mother Superior meets Army Drill Sergeant. Practical? Of course. Popular? Not so much.

Many women were turned away because they didn't fit Dix's strict criteria, stirring the pot of public opinion against her. Was she right in being so selective, putting professionalism over any romantic notions of wartime nursing? Or did she go too far? Ah, the age-old question of principle vs. practicality.

They say the road to hell is paved with good intentions, and Dix had her share of stumbles. Take the story of Mary Edwards Walker, a contract surgeon who ended up being the only woman to receive the Medal of Honor. Sounds like someone you'd want on your team, right? Well, not according to Dix, who took issue with Walker's insistence on wearing pants — yes, pants! In rejecting Walker's services, did Dix sacrifice competence at the altar of decorum? It's a moot point that stokes the embers of debate even today.

In The Crucible of War: Dix's Lasting Impact Despite The Storms

So, where does this leave us? Dix didn't come out of the Civil War smelling like a rose, let's be honest. She faced her share of criticisms, controversies, and obstacles. Yet, her role was pivotal. She wasn't just a cog in the war machine; she was the grease that kept it running, however imperfectly. Whether you see her as a flawed hero or a figure of controversy, one thing's for sure: Dorothea Dix left an indelible mark on military nursing.

Turning Pain into Progress: The Lessons of War

So what can we glean from all this? Was Dorothea Dix a saint, a sinner, or something else entirely? In the labyrinth of history, it's easy to get lost in the maze of good and bad decisions, triumphs, and setbacks. But one thing's for sure — Dix's time as Superintendent of Army Nurses wasn't just a series of black and white snapshots; it was a full-colour epic, replete with nuanced shades of grey.

The war did more than just test Dix's mettle; it refined it. Just as steel is forged in the furnace, so is her approach to mental health care. In the crucible of battle and disease, Dix saw firsthand the mental toll of war on soldiers and civilians alike. Though she had been advocating for the mentally ill long before the Civil War, the experiences, the controversies, the challenges — heck, even the failures — they all served as an intense 'masterclass,' shaping her later efforts in mental health reform.

Wrapping It Up A Legacy that Spans Beyond the Battlefield

Could you imagine going through what she did and coming out the other side without some chinks in the armour? Let's give credit where credit is due: Dorothea Dix changed the game. She took a system that was so flawed it made a house of cards look stable, and she turned it into something approaching functional.

She did not solve all the problems. And yes, she made mistakes along the way. But she'll be there when the ink dries on the pages of history, taking up more than her fair share of lines. Whether as an advocate for the mentally ill, a pivotal cog in the war machine, or a controversial figure who could ruffle feathers just by entering the room, Dix made her presence known.

So, what's the big takeaway? Heroes are made in a place other than vacuums. They're made in the messy, gritty reality we all inhabit. And sometimes, they come in the form of a stern woman who'd stare down a general if it meant saving just one more life. In the theatre of war, Dorothea Dix played her role, not without blemishes, but always with a determination that's as inspiring today as it was over a century ago.

Did Dix have her flaws? Absolutely. But let's ask ourselves this: Isn't the sum total of a person's deeds greater than any individual missteps? Dorothea Dix proves that even flawed heroes can change the world. So the next time you hear her name, remember the controversies and the thousands of lives she touched, both on and off the battlefield.

Challenges and controversies

And so we're left to ponder: How do we measure a life like Dorothea Dix's? Is it in the bills passed, the hospitals built, or the attitudes shifted? Sure, those things count. But what about the lives changed or even saved through her work in the Civil War, where she navigated a minefield of challenges and controversies?

Was she a perfect leader? Far from it. Her term as Superintendent of Army Nurses was mired in administrative mishaps and marred by some ill-judged decisions. Like the way she initially demanded that all nurses be over 30 and plain-looking, drawing ire and ridicule. Or her frequent run-ins with Army doctors, some of whom saw her not as an ally but as an obstacle.

Yet, how do you weigh those against her tireless commitment to improve conditions for wounded soldiers? Even her critics couldn't deny the results: better-organized hospitals, cleaner medical supplies, and — yes, a cadre of dedicated, well-trained nurses. You see, Dix may have been an imperfect leader, but she was a leader where it mattered most.

Behind the strict rules and the confrontational approach was an unwavering devotion to human dignity. Dix was not just concerned with the body but also with the soul. She wanted to lift the spirits of the wounded, to remind them of their humanity in a time when they felt anything but human.

Would we have chosen some of her methods? Probably not. But let's cut through the fog of war for a moment: Here was a woman who took on the system, pushed for reform, and left an indelible impact on mental health care that crossed national borders. Heck, she even locked horns with military brass in her unwavering mission to bring some decency to the hellishness of war.

The war years were but a chapter in Dix's extraordinary life. Her skills, flaws, ideals, and compromises were magnified in this high-stakes arena. After the war, she returned to her lifelong mission: advocating for the mentally ill. And guess what? The battles she fought during the Civil War served her well because she returned even more resilient, experienced, and determined than ever.

How often do we see a human being in such vivid colour, with all the complexities and contradictions that make us who we are? Dorothea Dix's journey, filled with triumphs and challenges, offers us a rare look into the struggles of a woman bent on changing the world. And while she didn't win every battle, she left behind a legacy that invites us all to be braver, more compassionate, and, yes, even more human.

Chapter 10

The Final Mile - Dix's Later Years

Isn't it ironic that a woman so devoted to the health of others had her battles to fight? Even as Dix aged, her health began deteriorating, raising concerns among those close to her. But should we be surprised? Given her work's physical and emotional toll, how could she not be affected? And yet, did she waver? Did she give up? Quite the opposite.

The decline in her health didn't deter her; it ignited an even deeper passion for her cause. She was like a candle burning at both ends, illuminating the darkness around her, even if it meant dwindling herself. In many ways, her failing health was the ultimate testament to her commitment. For Dix, the cause was more significant than the self, and she lived that philosophy until her last breath.

So, you've spent decades of your life fighting the good fight — championing the rights of the mentally ill, reshaping how society views them, advocating for change at the highest levels of government, and even managing a corps of nurses amid a civil war. What do you do for an encore? If you're Dorothea Dix, you keep pushing, that's what.

Retirement for Dorothea wasn't retirement. Think about it. This woman toured asylums across America and sailed across the Atlantic to do the same in Europe. Would she be content to sit back and sip tea for the rest of her days? Not a chance.

Dix continued her advocacy work well into her seventies, travelling across states to ensure that the hospitals she helped establish were up to snuff. Can you imagine? At an age when most people were reflecting on their lives, Dix was still out there, ensuring that the changes she had fought for were implemented and maintained. Why? Because for her, this was a lifelong commitment. Her work wasn't just a phase or a chapter in her life; it was her life.

Dix's later years saw her taking a particular interest in the New Jersey State Hospital at Trenton. Why New Jersey? Well, that's where she chose to make her final stand. This became her unique project, her last physical and emotional investment in a cause that had defined her entire adult life. Here, she spent her final years overseeing the hospital's operations and ensuring it lived up to her standards.

Retrospective of Her Impact

So, let's step back momentarily and ask: What did Dorothea Dix achieve? That's like asking what Beethoven achieved with his symphonies or what Van Gogh achieved with his paintings. Dix's work was transformational. It shifted societal norms and impacted legislation, sure. But its true impact was felt in the lives of the mentally ill individuals she saved from dark, dank cells and placed into caring institutions. She humanized them, fought for them, and, in the process, changed how a nation dealt with mental health.

Remember, she started as a school teacher with no medical background. Yet, she catalyzed a movement, crossing geographical and cultural barriers to sow the seeds of reform. Now, if that's not an impact, what is?

A Legacy of Light and Shadow: The Complex Tapestry of Dorothea Dix

No life is simple, and Dix's was no exception. She was a woman of contrasts — compassionate yet stern, influential yet controversial. She had her share of victories and setbacks, alliances and conflicts. But would you want it any other way? Isn't the tapestry of light and shadow making a life rich and instructive?

The Final Bow: Her Unseen Impact

Dix passed away in 1887, but don't you think for a second that her story ended there? Her work lived on, shaping mental health care not just in America but across the world. Institutions inspired by her vision continue to serve society to this day. And even when they fall short, they still stand as reminders of what one woman can achieve when armed with an indomitable will and an undying compassion.

In the end, isn't that the real story? A life filled with effort and meaning, victories and defeats, but an unwavering dedication to uplift those who could not uplift themselves. That's Dorothea Dix for you — a woman whose final mile was just as compelling as her first, leaving footprints too deep ever to be filled. How's that for a legacy?

The Sun Sets: Her Final Years in New Jersey

In the final stretch, Dix moved to the New Jersey State Hospital's guest quarters, the institution she had poured her later years into. Was it poetic justice, or just the circle of life coming to a close? Here was a woman who had spent a lifetime fighting for the dignity of the mentally ill, choosing to spend her last days in the environment she had transformed.

Wouldn't you find a deep sense of symmetry there? The very walls she fought to build and reform became her sanctuary, the ground she walked became her resting place, and the people she served became her final companions.

Unfinished Symphony: The Work That Continues

Who picks up the torch when a giant falls? Dix's passing left a void, no doubt about that. But it also left a blueprint, a vision that others could follow. Her work, deeply embedded in the system she helped create, became the curriculum for future reformers. And guess what? They did follow.

Could she have imagined the ripple effect of her work? The cascade of changes in mental health care that flowed from her initial plunge into the troubled waters of social justice? Maybe not. But just like a symphony doesn't stop at the last note but lingers in the air and hearts of the listeners, her impact reverberated long after she was gone.

Summing it All Up: What Do We Make of Dorothea Dix?

So here we are, tracing the contours of a life that defies easy summarization. A life that broke barriers, crossed oceans, challenged conventions, and, yes, had its fair share of controversies and setbacks. What are we to make of Dorothea Dix?

Imagine throwing a stone into a still pond. The ripples it creates spread out, affecting every water molecule in that pond. Dix's life was that stone, and the world of mental health care was the pond. The ripples she created are still expanding, affecting lives today.

She could have been better. But boy, did she make a difference. And in the end, isn't that what life is all about — making a difference? Dorothea Dix took on that challenge, molding it into a legacy that neither time nor tide can wash away. How will you make a difference? How will you cast your stone into the pond? That dear reader, is the question Dix leaves us with — a challenge that echoes through time, waiting for the next brave soul to answer the call.

The Twilight Symphony: Dix's Unseen Influence in Her Later Years

So, you've heard about the lioness in her prime—how she roared and the world listened. But what about when the roar softened when the lioness aged? Did Dix fade into the background, her work complete? Hardly. Let's talk about her final chapter, a blend of rest, reflection, and, yes, unrelenting influence.

Still, a Force to Reckon With Quiet Power in Her Final Days

Think of a mighty river flowing into a calm lake. The force is still there; it's just distributed differently. Dorothea Dix didn't stop advocating for the mentally ill; she shifted her focus. She returned to the institutions she helped create, spending her final years at Trenton State Hospital in New Jersey. But did she settle down? Can a force of nature ever truly be tamed?

Dix kept correspondence with various officials, healthcare providers, and reformers until the end. She wanted to know how the policies were working or not working. She'd fire off letters, sometimes sharp, sometimes encouraging, but always insightful. So, why bother? Simple: The fight for reform didn't end with her, and she knew it.

The Passing of the Torch: Inspiring the Next Wave of Advocates

Have you ever considered what kind of mark you'll leave on this world? Dix did. And she didn't just leave behind buildings or laws; she left behind people — trained, inspired, passionate people. They were the next wave of advocates who would carry on her mission. Isn't authentic leadership about preparing the next generation to take the reins?

Through her work, Dix indirectly trained a cadre of mental healthcare professionals. Even in her final days, her correspondence was an educational tool, providing those following her footsteps with the insights and fortitude to face the challenges ahead.

Her legacy in the modern era

So, what's the big picture? What does Dorothea Dix mean to us today, living in an era so far removed from her own? Let's get one thing straight: The landscape of mental health care may have evolved, but the foundations remain the same.

Ever heard of Nellie Bly, the journalist who went undercover in an asylum and blew the lid off the abhorrent conditions? Guess who inspired her? Or how about the National Alliance on Mental Illness (NAMI), a grassroots organization dedicated to improving the lives of the mentally ill? Well, they stand on Dix's shoulders.

And it's not just in America. Think about how our understanding and treatment of mental health have changed globally. The United Nations recognizes mental health as a global concern. Nonprofits are working in low-income countries to provide mental health resources. Where do you think the inspiration for these monumental shifts came from? Yep, you guessed it—Dorothea Dix.

Planting Seeds for the Future: What's the Takeaway?

Is it fair to say Dorothea Dix was a visionary? Absolutely. But what's the point of vision if it dies with you? Dix ensured her vision would outlive her. And boy, has it ever. Through tireless efforts, she elevated mental health care from a medieval nightmare to an institution of empathy and science. She laid the groundwork for a future she'd never seen.

So, what do you think her legacy means for us? Isn't it a challenge? If one woman, born in an era when women were not even considered full citizens, could revolutionize how society treats its most vulnerable, what's our excuse? Dorothea Dix shows us that you don't need to see the end of the road to take the first step. You need the courage to believe that your steps matter and are part of a more extensive journey.

In the end, Dorothea Dix didn't just build hospitals; she built a legacy that we are all a part of, whether we realize it or not. So the question is more than what Dix did, but what we will do. How will we contribute to this never-ending story of compassion, reform, and basic human decency? That, my friends, is the challenge that Dorothea Dix leaves us with — a legacy not set in stone but as dynamic and evolving as the human spirit.

Walking in Her Footsteps: Dix's Legacy in Modern Mental Health Activism

Have you ever walked through a forest and wondered about the roots under your feet? They spread far and wide, connecting trees in an intricate, life-giving network. In the same way, the roots Dix laid down in the 19th century still nourish the tree of mental health advocacy today. But how does her influence manifest in our lives now? How does her legacy filter through the noise of a world cluttered with social and political strife?

It starts with education. Consider how our perspectives on mental health have changed over the years. In schools across the globe, there's now a focused effort to integrate mental health into the curriculum. Kids are taught empathy and understanding, words that were rarely if ever, associated with asylums in Dix's day. Now, isn't it something to realise that the seeds she planted have grown into this?

The Wider Cultural Shift: Stigma and Acceptance

Do you remember when discussing mental health was taboo? Even a few decades ago, this was a subject that families swept under the rug. Not anymore. Mental health is part of the national, even global, conversation today. Celebrities and influencers open up about their struggles, and it's considered brave rather than scandalous. Would this openness be possible without Dix's foundational work?

Her legacy also lives on in legislation. Policies and reforms that protect the rights of mental health patients aren't just conceived out of the blue; they are the product of generations of advocacy. If Dix were here to see the Americans with Disabilities Act, one must wonder if she would smile. Would she say, "This is what I fought for"? We'll never know, but imagining she wouldn't feel a sense of triumph is hard.

Innovations and Backlashes: The Ongoing Fight

But let's not kid ourselves. The journey is still ongoing; it's far from complete. The institutions Dix fought so hard to reform can sometimes fall short. Scandals erupt; institutions are criticised, sometimes justly, sometimes not. Why does this matter? Because it means the fight she began is still ours to continue. Progress, as we know, isn't a straight line. There are bumps and regressions, and each one serves as a wake-up call: Dix's work, our work, is not done.

The Challenge Awaits: How Will You Join the Fight?

So here's the big question: What are you going to do? What am I going to do? Dorothea Dix, born in 1802, set a course that we're still following. You're carrying on her legacy when you advocate for mental health awareness and treat others with the dignity and respect they deserve. Sure, you and I are not building asylums or lobbying Congress. But we're adding to the conversation, changing attitudes one person at a time.

So let's not mince words: The challenge is daunting, perhaps now more than ever. But isn't that the essence of legacy — to inspire others to take up the cause, even when the odds seem insurmountable?

In the final reckoning, Dorothea Dix's life is not just a historical account of an extraordinary woman. It's a guidebook, a blueprint for action. Her legacy is not in the bricks and mortar of institutions but in the evolving societal perspectives and humane policies that govern us today.

When we talk about Dorothea Dix, we're not just talking about a woman who lived two centuries ago but about us, here and now. What we choose to do with her legacy — how we choose to understand and value mental health — will define our present and future. Are you ready to be a part of that? Because I know I am.

People and circumstances that contributed to her journey

Life is a string of moments, relationships, and events. Dorothea Lynde Dix, synonymous with mental health reform in America, didn't etch her legacy in a vacuum. Let's dive into the colourful mosaic of people and circumstances that gave contour and depth to her path. Who were the hands that held the chisel as Dix sculpted her destiny? What were the winds that steered her sails?

The Early Seed: Family Background

The Dix household wasn't your picturesque, all-American family. Born in 1802 in Hampden, Maine, young Dorothea faced hardships many of us cannot imagine. Her father, Joseph Dix, was an itinerant preacher. The word 'itinerant' is telling. The man was restless, and his family was steeped in instability. And her mother? She battled with depression. The cruel irony is that Dorothea's earliest exposure to mental health challenges was at home. Could the early friction of her home life act like the sandpaper, shaping her into the advocate she became?

The Helping Hand: William Ellery Channing

The importance of mentors can't be overstated. For Dix, that figure was William Ellery Channing, a Unitarian minister. Remember, this was the 19th century when education for women wasn't a given. Yet, Channing saw potential in her, providing her access to his library and fostering her love for education. What's a mind without the kindling of knowledge, anyway?

The Shaping Years: Teaching and Education

Dix was a teacher before she was an advocate. Sounds like a detour. But what if I told you it was a training ground? Through her experiences, especially at her Boston school for girls, she honed her knack for empathy and organisation — which later became her cornerstones. She was crafting her toolset, even if she didn't know it yet.

The Tide-Changing Event: The East Cambridge Jail Visit

Some moments in life are like forks on the road, wouldn't you agree? For Dix, a visit to the East Cambridge Jail was her fork — a shocking eye-opener. She found inmates with mental illness huddled in squalid, inhumane conditions. The horror of it fueled her, igniting her into action. Could she have ignored it? Sure. But some knots need to be untangled, not sidestepped.

The Power Duo: Samuel Gridley Howe and Horace Mann

Do you know those friendships that are more than just casual Saturday night dinners? Dix found allies in Samuel Gridley Howe and Horace Mann, two pioneers in social reform. Together, they formed a reformist trifecta. While Howe was focused on education for the visually impaired, and Mann was a leading voice in public education, their paths met in their collective passion for societal betterment. Three separate rivers converge to form a powerful, unstoppable current.

The Bumps on the Road: Resistance and Criticism

No one said fighting against the grain would be smooth sailing. Dix faced resistance from the public, lawmakers, and even within the medical community. These hurdles weren't just obstacles but catalysts that pushed her to fine-tune her strategies. Opposition often paves the way for stronger conviction.

The Final Phase: Fading Health and Unwavering Commitment

In her later years, Dix's health started to deteriorate. It's one of life's cruel jokes. The caregiver needs care. Yet, her fading physical health never diluted her commitment. She continued her work, albeit slower, redefining what it means to be "retired." It's like a candle burning brightest just before it goes out.

What's the Takeaway? Lessons From a Life Richly Lived

So, what's the fabric of a life like Dorothea Dix's made of? It's a tapestry woven from various threads—family, mentors, career choices, allies, and even adversaries. Each played its part, adding a unique texture to her life.

The compelling question that lingers is: How do we let the people and circumstances in our lives shape us? Do we see them as stepping stones or recognize them as the sculptor's hands, molding us into who we're meant to be?

If Dorothea Dix teaches us anything, life's influences aren't just pieces in a mosaic; they're the colors that make the artwork worth staring at, studying, and perhaps most importantly, remembering.

Notes And References

Where The Story Meets The Street

You know how, in detective shows, the investigator pins various newspaper clippings, photos, and pieces of evidence to a corkboard? They connect the dots with red strings, aiming to solve the mystery. Our journey through Dorothea Lynde Dix's life has been like that. Now it's time to look at our corkboard — the notes and references that make the story rich, believable, and verifiable.

The Cornerstones: Primary Sources

Primary sources are like the eyewitnesses in a courtroom drama. They were there. They saw it happen. And in the case of Dorothea Dix, we're talking about her writings, the bills she drafted, and the letters she penned. Have you ever read something in someone's handwriting and felt you could hear their voice in your head? That's what going through Dix's letters is like—a direct hotline to the past.

The Memorial

One standout document is her "Memorial," presented to the Massachusetts legislature in 1843. This was not just a document; it was a rallying cry. Picture Martin Luther nailing his theses to the church door; this was Dix's saying, "Enough is enough."

The Sidekicks: Secondary Sources

If primary sources are the star quarterback, secondary sources are the teammates who help carry the game. Books, academic papers, and documentaries about Dix provide us with the analysis, the why's and how's behind the what's. They're like a good sportscaster, making sense of the plays and strategies we've just witnessed.

Dorothea Dix: New England Reformer

Jane E. Schultz's book on Dix is illuminating. Suppose you've ever read a biography that tells a life story and puts it into the larger context of the world in which that person lived. In that case, you'll get what Schultz accomplishes here.

Eyewitnesses: Accounts from Contemporaries

Dix didn't operate in a vacuum. She was surrounded by a cast of characters that would make any period drama green with envy. Think of these accounts as interviews in a documentary film — each adds another layer to the story.

Letters and Journals

The letters and journals from those who worked with her or were affected by her reforms add colour and depth to the narrative. Ever read a letter from an old friend, and suddenly you're back in another time and place? These firsthand accounts work like that; they take you to the heart of the 19th century alongside Dix and her contemporaries.

Contemporary Commentary: Op-Eds and Essays

Imagine you're watching a movie, and suddenly, it pauses for a quick explainer video, helping you understand the complex plot. Essays and opinion pieces from her time act in a similar way. They don't just describe what happened; they explain the significance, like a director's commentary on a DVD.

Newspaper Archives

Remember to underestimate the power of the press. Newspapers from Dix's time serve as a social barometer. They show how her work was received, both the cheers and the jeers. It's like reading online comments below an article—immediate, raw, and often divisive.

Printed in Great Britain
by Amazon